What's in a Cave?

Keith Fay

INFOMAX COMMON CORE READERS

Rosen Classroom™

New York

Published in 2014 by The Rosen Publishing Group, Inc.
29 East 21st Street, New York, NY 10010

Book Design: Jon D'Rozario

Photo Credits: Cover SSokolov/Shutterstock.com; p. 5 Vitalii Nesterchuk/Shutterstock.com; p. 7 (sea cave) zebra0209/ Shutterstock.com; p. 7 (ice cave) Armin Rose/Shutterstock.com; p. 7 (lava cave) Radoslaw Lecyk/Shutterstock.com; p. 9 Sarun T/Shutterstock.com; pp. 11, 15 (stalactites) George Allen Penton/Shutterstock.com; p. 13 Sergemi/ Shutterstock.com; p. 15 (stalagmites) Dumitrescu Ciprian-Florin/Shutterstock.com; p. 17 (shelfstone) Alexey Stiop/ Shutterstock.com; p.17 (cave popcorn) salajean/Shutterstock.com; p. 17 (column) LazarevaEl/Shutterstock.com; p. 17 (flowstone) Hemera/Thinkstock.com; p. 19 Meaning/Shutterstock.com; p. 21 gremlin/E+/Getty Images; p. 22 Eduardo Rivero/Shutterstock.com.

ISBN: 978-1-4777-2321-0
6-pack ISBN: 978-1-4777-2322-7

Manufactured in the United States of America

CPSIA Compliance Information: Batch #CS13RC: For further information contact Rosen Publishing, New York, New York at 1-800-237-9932.

Contents

Discovering Caves

Caves are hidden worlds filled with cool rock **formations** and animals that can live in total darkness. There are millions of caves on Earth, and each cave took millions of years to form. Life inside caves is very different from life outside of them.

People can discover what's inside caves by going caving, or spelunking (spih-LUNG-king).

When caving is done safely, it's an activity that can help people learn about the hidden world inside caves.

Special Kinds of Caves

There are many different kinds of caves. Ice caves can be found in huge pieces of ice called glaciers. Sea caves are made when ocean waves crash against cliffs and wear away the rock.

Lava caves are found near **volcanoes**. These caves are made of melted rock, which is known as lava. When the lava on the edges hardens faster than flowing lava at the center, it **creates** a cave.

Each type of cave looks different because it's formed in a different way.

ice cave

lava cave

sea cave

7

How Does a Cave Form?

The most common type of cave is formed under Earth's **surface**. This happens when rainwater breaks down rocks over millions of years, creating caves.

The kind of land that caves form in is called karst. It's made up of rock that's easily broken down over time. One kind of rock that's usually found in caves is called limestone.

Limestone is a soft kind of rock, which makes it great for creating caves.

Caves form in karst when rainwater goes through cracks in the rock. This water contains a gas called carbon dioxide (KAHR-buhn dy-AHK-syd). When this gas mixes with water, it forms an acid. Acid is a kind of **liquid** that burns away things or breaks them down. This acid slowly breaks down the rock it travels through.

The acid that broke down these rocks wasn't very strong. That's why it takes such a long time for caves to form!

After millions of years, the karst breaks down, leaving **hollow** areas under Earth's surface. These areas join together over time to form one big cave!

Rainwater still drips into the cave from the ground above. When it dries, it leaves behind minerals. A mineral is somthing solid that's found in nature but isn't living. Minerals create the rock formations in a cave.

The rock formations in a cave get their colors from the minerals that created them.

Rocks Around the Cave

When water dries on the top, or roof, of the cave, it creates rock formations that hang down. These are called stalactites (stuh-LAK-tyts). The water can also drip from the roof of the cave to the floor. The minerals left behind on the floor of the cave make rock formations that grow up from the ground. These are called stalagmites (stuh-LAG-myts).

Sometimes, these rock formations can grow together to make one large formation, called a column. Columns reach from the floor of a cave to its roof.

stalactites

stalagmites

What other rock formations can you find in a cave? Shelfstone forms around pools of water in a cave or places where pools used to be. This flat rock formation shows how high water can get in a cave.

Cave popcorn is found in many different places inside a cave, such as the walls, floor, and even other rock formations. It looks just like the popcorn we eat!

Caves are full of cool rock formations!

Cool Cave Formations

column
Stalagmite and stalactite grow together.

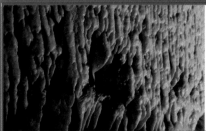

flowstone
Water runs over rocks in the cave.

cave popcorn
Water splashes in a cave.

shelfstone
Minerals build up around cave pools.

What Lives in a Cave?

You can find many different animals in a cave. Some live near the front. They use the cave as a home but need light and food from the outside, too. These animals include bears, foxes, and skunks.

Bats also use caves to sleep in during the day. They often hang from the roofs of caves when they sleep. At night, they leave the caves to hunt for food.

Bats live in groups called colonies.

Some animals spend their whole life inside a cave! These animals, called troglobites, have changed over time to be able to live in total darkness. Many of them are blind because they don't need to see in the darkest parts of caves. These animals include certain kinds of fish and lizards. There are some insects and spiders that only live deep in caves, too.

The olm is a blind animal that lives in the darkest part of some caves. It can go several years without eating!

Cave Paintings

In some caves, you can even find works of art! There are paintings in caves around the world made by humans thousands of years ago.

So many cool things can be found in caves. It's fun to learn about these hidden worlds!

Many cave paintings include animals, such as horses and deer.

Glossary

create (kree-AYT) To make something.

formation (fohr-MAY-shun) Shape.

hollow (HAH-loh) Having empty space inside.

liquid (LIH-kwuhd) Something that flows freely like water.

surface (SUHR-fuhs) The top part of something that can be seen.

volcano (vahl-KAY-noh) An opening in Earth's surface through which hot, liquid rock sometimes flows.

Index